# The Al...
*a play...*
## John F...

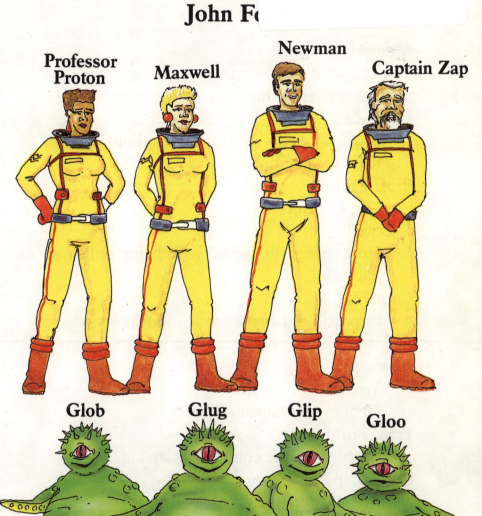

Nelson

*In the spaceship Adventurer.*

**Maxwell**
There's a planet coming up on the scanner, Captain.
**Capt. Zap**
Professor, see what you can find out about it from the computer.
**Prof. Proton**
Yes, Captain.
**Maxwell**
How strange! It seems we're being pulled into orbit.
**Capt. Zap**
Impossible! Let me see . . . Great Scott! You're right. Newman, fire reverse rockets.
**Newman**
Yes, sir . . . Sir, they're not working! We seem to be drained of power.
**Prof. Proton**
Nothing on the computer, Captain.
**Capt. Zap**
Are you sure?
**Prof. Proton**
Positive.

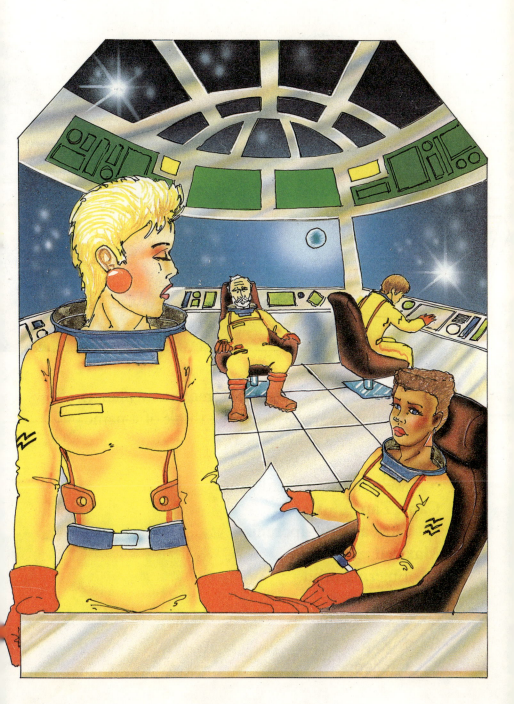

**Capt. Zap**
    It looks like we've discovered a new planet. We'll be famous. We must think of a name for it.

**Newman**
    We're out of control, sir!

**Capt. Zap**
    How about Zaporania?

**Maxwell**
    Entering orbit.

**Newman**
    Power's gone!

**Capt. Zap**
    Or Zappo?

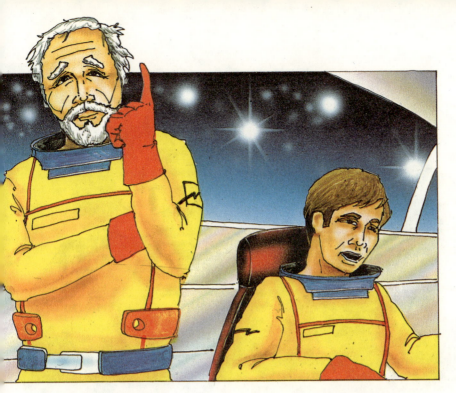

**Maxwell**
>There's nothing we can do. We're in orbit around the planet.

**Capt. Zap**
>Zapania, perhaps?

**Prof. Proton**
>Captain Zap, what are we to do?

**Capt. Zap**
>Land, of course.

**Prof. Proton**
>But there's no power.

**Capt. Zap**
>No power? Where's it gone? Why didn't anyone tell me?

*On the planet.*

**Glob**
  The ship is circling the planet.
**Glug**
  The welcome party is ready.
**Glob**
  Do you think they will be friendly? They might put up a fight.
**Glug**
  My dear Glob, why should they do that? We wish them no harm. As soon as they see our tentacles outstretched in friendship they will know we are no danger to them.
**Glob**
  I hope you're right. I couldn't bear it if anything happened to our dear comrades who are going out to meet them. If anything beastly was to happen, well, I don't know what I would do.
**Glug**
  Now, now, please don't cry, old friend. I'm sure everything will be all right. Ah, here's Glip.

*Glip enters.*

**Glip**

Is everything ready for our visitors?
Is it time to go out and meet them yet? I'm getting very impatient. So are the others.

**Glug**

Not long to wait now. The spacecraft is on its way to the surface. As soon as we know exactly where they have landed you can all go off and look for them.

**Glob**

Please be careful, Glip.

**Glip**
>Careful? There's nothing to fear. As soon as they see the feast we've prepared for them they will be our friends for ever. We have jellied toad in acorn sauce; nettle and eggshell salad; fried wood chips . . . I can't wait.

**Glob**
>I suppose you're right. It is about time we made contact with people from other planets.

**Glug**
>That's it, Glob. No good being silly old stick-in-the-muds. We have to move with the times.

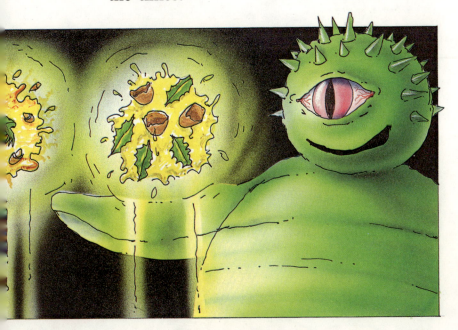

*In the spaceship.*

**Capt. Zap**
> You mean to say that you can find absolutely nothing wrong with the ship?

**Maxwell**
> That's right, sir. Everything appears to be in perfect order.

**Capt. Zap**
> Then how do you explain the fact that we have no power?

*Silence.*

> . . . Well?

**Maxwell**
> I can't, sir.

**Capt. Zap**
> Then check everything again, and a third time if necessary. Really! I can't stand incompetence.

**Prof. Proton**
> Captain, might I make a suggestion? It is possible that the ship is being influenced by something outside.

**Capt. Zap**
> From down there, you mean?

**Prof. Proton**
> It is possible.

**Capt. Zap**
>Then let's go down and take a look.

**Prof. Proton**
>But we have no power.

**Capt. Zap**
>Oh, no . . . I forgot.

**Newman**
>Captain! Power is returning. It's not much, but we definitely have some power.

**Capt. Zap**
>Enough to land, Newman?

**Newman**
>Just about, sir.

**Capt. Zap**
>Then take us down.

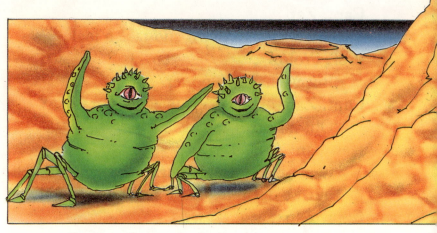

*On the planet, the welcoming party is on its way.*

**Glip**
> The ship from Earth has landed on the other side of the hill. It shouldn't take long for us to get there.

**Gloo**
> I wonder what they look like?

**Glip**
> We shall all know soon, dear boy.

**Gloo**
> Exciting, isn't it?

**Glip**
> Great fun, and a great day for all of us. Come on, let's hurry to meet them.

**Gloo**
> I'll race you . . .

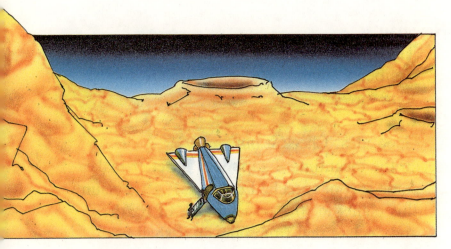

*On the ship.*

**Newman**
> A perfect landing, sir.

**Capt. Zap**
> Excellent! Do you see any aliens?

**Newman**
> None visible, sir.

**Capt. Zap**
> Good. Arm yourselves, just in case. Make sure you have your laser guns and, Maxwell, bring the high energy cannon.

**Prof. Proton**
> It sounds like you're expecting trouble, Captain.

**Capt. Zap**
> Better safe than sorry, Professor, that's my motto. Now, let's go!

*They get out of the ship.*

**Newman**

There's a tall rock over there, Captain. If I climbed to the top I'd be able to see a long way.

**Capt. Zap**

Good idea. Check it out.

In the meantime, I suppose I'd better make some sort of speech. Let me see . . . I claim this planet for the space empire of Earth, and declare that from now on it shall be known as Zaponia after its discoverer.

*The crew clap.*

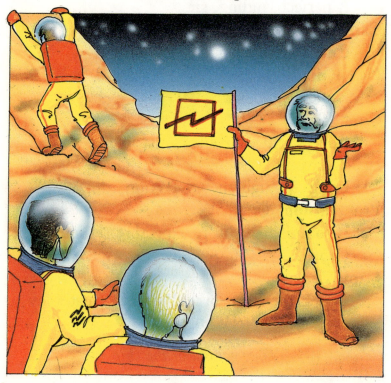

**Prof. Proton**
>Do you see anything, Newman?
>Newman! Are you all right?. . . Newman!

**Newman**
>Captain! Captain! They're horrible!

**Prof. Proton**
>Calm down, man. What are horrible?

**Newman**
>Aliens. They're huge! They've got arms like an octopus; bulbous spiky heads with one enormous pink eye. Urg! Their skin is like an elephant's, but slimy! Quick! Let's get away. They've got six spidery legs . . . and . . . and they're coming this way!

**Capt. Zap**
>Aliens, my foot! We'll show them who's boss around here. Behind the rock, everyone. Guns ready. Take aim, but don't fire until I tell you.

**Maxwell**

Here they come.

**Capt. Zap**

Remember, hold your fire until the signal.

**Prof. Proton**

But Captain, don't you think we should . . .

**Maxwell**

Newman was right – they're hideous.

**Prof. Proton**

Captain, I must advise you to give them a chance.

**Capt. Zap**

And be eaten alive? No thanks! Take aim, everyone . . .

3 – 2 – 1

FIRE!